WAR IN THE
PERSIAN GULF

Fred Bratman

THE MILLBROOK PRESS
Brookfield, Connecticut

Published by The Millbrook Press
2 Old New Milford Road
Brookfield, CT 06804
© 1991 Blackbirch Graphics, Inc.

Created and produced in association with Blackbirch Graphics.
Series Editor: Bruce S. Glassman

5 4 3

Library of Congress Cataloging-in-Publication Data
Bratman, Fred.
War in the Persian Gulf / Fred Bratman. — 1st ed.
p. cm. — (Headliners)
Includes bibliographical references and index.
Summary: Discusses the Persian Gulf crisis, from the Iraqi
invasion of Kuwait in 1990 to the Allied victory in 1991.
ISBN 1-56294-051-1 (lib. bdg.)
1. Persian Gulf War, 1991 — Juvenile literature. [1. Persian Gulf
War, 1991. 2. Iraq-Kuwait Crisis, 1990.] I. Title. II. Series.
DS79.72.B73 1991
956.704'3 — dc20   91-38535   CIP   AC

For Elsa, Anne, and Jarah

Contents

 Chapter One/ Arab Against Arab   5

 Chapter Two/ Oil: Fuel for the World   13

 Chapter Three/ The Birthplace of Western Civilization   21

 Chapter Four/ The U.S. and the U.N. Take Action   31

 Chapter Five/ Desert Shield Becomes Desert Storm   41

Chronology   61

For Further Reading   62

Index   62

Chapter 1

Arab Against Arab

Iraq overruns an old, helpless, but once valuable ally

By breakfast time the invasion was over. Iraq had seized Kuwait.

In the predawn hours of August 2, 1990, Iraqi forces swept south across the border into the tiny Persian Gulf country. In six hours Iraqi tanks, missiles, artillery and jeeps fulfilled a long-held dream of Iraq's President Saddam Hussein: control of oil-rich Kuwait. For years Saddam had his eye on his neighbor, and now its wealth was his.

The strategy was simple. The first wave of 30,000 Iraqi troops converged from three directions. They raced to the capital, Kuwait City, capturing airports and military barracks along the way.

As the ground forces advanced, Iraqi warplanes bombed key targets around Kuwait City. Once in the capital, Iraqi troops rushed to the royal palaces, where the ruling family lived. They wanted to capture Emir Jabir al-Ahmad al-Sabah, Kuwait's ruler, in his sleep. But the emir was awake, trying to rally his forces and keep the country from falling into Iraqi hands.

Kuwait's small army tried to defend against its powerful neighbor, but it was no match for Saddam's forces, toughened in an eight-year war with another neighbor, Iran.

The situation was hopeless, and the emir and many of his relatives and advisers fled in a motorcade that took them to refuge in neighboring Saudi Arabia.

Opposite:
Iraqi tanks roll into Kuwait in the early morning hours of August 2, 1990. Kuwaiti television broadcast the invasion as it occurred.

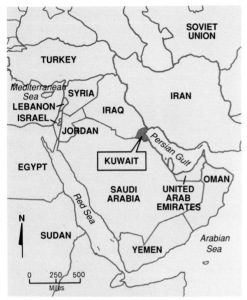

KUWAIT AND THE MIDDLE EAST

With the Iraqi army in control of the capital, Saddam sent 70,000 more troops into Kuwait, which is only about the size of the state of Connecticut. They moved south, toward the border with Saudi Arabia. By late Friday, a little more than 24 hours after the start of the invasion, more than 100,000 Iraqi troops were in Kuwait and many were massed on the Kuwait-Saudi Arabia border.

The invasion caught Saudi Arabia, the Persian Gulf's most oil-rich nation, off guard. It had reason to fear that it could be next in line. If Saddam had visions of controlling world oil supplies, Saudi Arabia would be the top prize. What's more, despite years of purchasing expensive, sophisticated military equipment, the Saudis were no match for the Iraqis.

The World Reacts

The reaction from the United States and much of the rest of the world was swift and blunt. President George Bush called the invasion "naked aggression."

The United Nations Security Council voted overwhelmingly to condemn Iraq's actions. The council demanded that Iraqi troops withdraw immediately from Kuwait. Most European nations also condemned Iraq and banned trade with the country.

Also within hours of the invasion, President Bush froze Iraq's assets in the United States, such as money in banks. He sent more U.S. warships to join six that had been on duty in the Gulf since July.

The United States had not yet sent ground troops, nor was it in a military position to invade Iraq. But President Bush made it clear that he would live up to the promises of two earlier presidents to come to the aid of Saudi Arabia, if it was attacked.

The Arab World Splits

Arab nations, too were outraged. For years, Arab leaders had argued that the greatest threat to peace in the region was Israel, which had been established as a Jewish homeland in 1948. There is a long history of bitter conflict between Israel and its Arab neighbors. The Arabs object to Israel's continued control of areas it won from Arab countries in the Six Day War in 1967. And they continue to say that Palestinian Arabs in those regions have been treated unfairly. But now, the biggest source of trouble was Iraq, a member of the Arab community.

Above:
Sheik Jabir al-Ahmad al-Sabah, the leader of Kuwait.
Left: Saddam Hussein, president of Iraq.

Many Arab leaders had preached pan-Arabism, the idea that although borders separated them, all Arabs shared a common history, culture, and language. Now, Saddam had undermined the foundation of pan-Arabism with his attack on fellow Arabs.

In the Arab world, emotions following the Iraqi attack moved from disbelief to shock to anger. Many Arab leaders were reluctant at first to speak out against a fellow Arab. They hoped that Saddam would quickly withdraw his troops. But that did not happen.

Instead, Iraqi troops seized absolute control of Kuwait. They executed scores of people and abused thousands

Opposite:
A South Carolina National Guard member says a final goodbye to his daughter before leaving for active duty in the Persian Gulf.

U.S. President George Bush addresses the country in August of 1990 about the role America will play in the Persian Gulf conflict.

more. They looted banks and stole hospital and military equipment and shipped it back to Iraq. They raped women and threw frail, elderly people out of old-age homes.

The first Arab leader to condemn the invasion was Egypt's President Hosni Mubarak. He demanded that Iraq immediately withdraw its forces from Kuwait. In recent years, Egypt has taken positions unpopular in the Middle East. It is the only Arab nation to have signed a peace treaty with Israel. All others have been sworn enemies of Israel since its creation. The Camp David Accords of 1978 brought an official peace between the two nations. Since then, Egypt has become less suspicious of the non-Arab world. It has also strengthened its ties with the United States.

Jordan Tries to Aid Peace

At first, other Arab nations were more reluctant to speak out against Iraq. In some cases, they feared Iraq's military might. They also cited the need to uphold Arab unity.

Jordan, Iraq's neighbor to the west, steered a tight course of neutrality. Jordan's King Hussein (no relation to Saddam Hussein) feared that Iraq might invade or stir up trouble that would topple him from power. King Hussein's grip on the throne was seen as weak. More than 50 percent of the people in Jordan are Palestinians, and in the past this group's grievances have led to bloody violence. Indeed, many Palestinians supported Iraq's invasion. Thus, soon after the invasion, King Hussein sought to play the role of peacemaker. He traveled to Baghdad, Iraq's capital, to Europe, and even to President Bush's vacation home in Kennebunkport, Maine. But the king's mission failed. Saddam vowed to hold onto Kuwait.

Meanwhile, the key player had yet to be heard from. Saudi Arabia said little in the hours following the invasion. The country, ruled by the Saud clan, is usually cautious in its political actions. At first, King Fahd held back from condemning the invasion. But once it became clear his

King Fahd of Saudi Arabia requested help from the United States as soon as he learned his country was in danger of being invaded by Iraq.

King Hussein of Jordan, who tried in vain to play peacemaker in the final weeks before the war began.

kingdom could be next, he spoke out and requested U.S. troops.

The United States responded quickly, speeding troops and equipment to the region. At the same time, other nations joined the military effort. From Europe, Britain and France sent troops. From the Arab world, Egypt and Syria dispatched soldiers. This created a multinational force prepared to defend Saudi Arabia from Iraqi invasion.

The strong response to the invasion seemed to come as a surprise to Saddam. He expected only talk—no serious opposition to his military moves. But too much of the world depended on the vast oil resources that lie under the deserts of the Middle East to treat the invasion lightly.

11

Chapter 2

Oil: Fuel for the World

P resident Bush cited oil as one major cause for the United States' actions. Secretary of State James Baker was even more direct. He told Congress that if Iraq were allowed to keep Kuwait's vast oil fields, the world economy would be in peril.

Oil has long been called black gold because it is so precious. The world runs on oil, and without it the business of many countries would come to a grinding halt. Oil is needed to fuel cars, trucks, and planes, but it is also vital in manufacturing, particularly as a raw material for chemicals. These chemicals are used to make plastic soft drink bottles, paints, and even lipstick.

Oil is needed in dozens of other ways. That is why a shortage of oil always hurts any nation's economy. Within a few days of the Iraqi invasion of Kuwait, the price of gasoline, one of the many products made from oil, jumped by 50 percent.

The United States is accustomed to cheap oil and uses an average of 25 barrels of oil per person a year. (There are 42 gallons in a barrel.) That is twice as much as France or Britain, and much more than poorer countries such as China or Kenya.

Control of the world's richest petroleum resources has given great power to many nations in the Middle East

Opposite:
A Kuwaiti oil worker stands in front of a rig that pumps crude oil up from deep below the sands of the desert.

Oil Becomes a Weapon

In 1973, the Arab nations cut off sales of oil to the United States and other Western nations as punishment for supporting Israel after an attack by Egypt and Syria. In the United States, the oil embargo led to long lines at gas stations, and to hard economic times.

In 1979, Iran and other oil states once again tried to use oil to shape the Middle East policies of the United States. This time, the price of oil nearly doubled to $34 a barrel. It was then that President Jimmy Carter vowed to cut American dependency on foreign oil. The nation turned

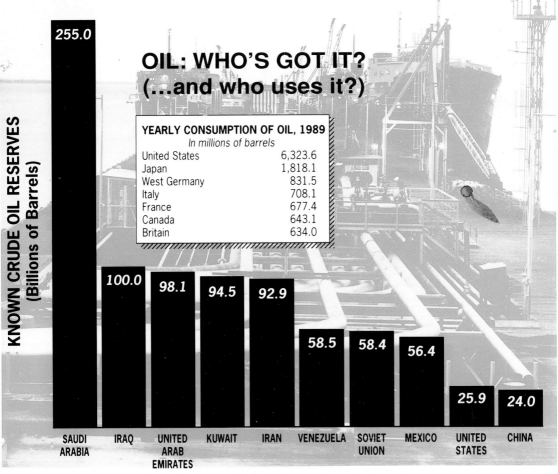

OIL: WHO'S GOT IT?
(...and who uses it?)

KNOWN CRUDE OIL RESERVES (Billions of Barrels)

Country	Reserves
SAUDI ARABIA	255.0
IRAQ	100.0
UNITED ARAB EMIRATES	98.1
KUWAIT	94.5
IRAN	92.9
VENEZUELA	58.5
SOVIET UNION	58.4
MEXICO	56.4
UNITED STATES	25.9
CHINA	24.0

YEARLY CONSUMPTION OF OIL, 1989
In millions of barrels

United States	6,323.6
Japan	1,818.1
West Germany	831.5
Italy	708.1
France	677.4
Canada	643.1
Britain	634.0

Information based on data from *Oil and Gas Journal*, (12/25/89); Energy Information Association; Population Reference Bureau.

down thermostats and reduced the speed limit on highways to save fuel. Carter also pushed development of such alternative energy sources as solar and nuclear power and other renewable fuels.

But a few years later, once the 1979 crisis was forgotten, the United States was again addicted to cheap oil. The government dropped exploration of new energy sources.

The price of oil dropped in the 1980s and the United States became more dependent on it. In 1970, imports

Cars in New Jersey line up for miles during the gas shortage of 1979. World supply was cut by OPEC during that year in an effort to increase prices and profits.

Kuwait: Oil-Rich Oasis

Before the Iraqi invasion, Kuwait prided itself on its wise use of billions of dollars it earned from oil, turning itself from a desert wilderness into a modern state. Less than 50 years ago, Kuwait was isolated from much of the world. But the discovery and exploitation of oil made Kuwait a tempting victim for Saddam Hussein to grab.

Kuwait was first settled in the early 1700s by one of the Arab tribes that wandered the desert. About 50 years later, the tribe elected the head of the al-Sabah family to rule it. The current emir traces his roots back to that original desert chieftain.

The British were the first European power to take an interest in Kuwait, using it as a stop on a major trade route. In 1899, Kuwait accepted British protection as a means of avoiding domination by the Ottoman Empire. In 1914, Britain recognized Kuwait as independent from the Ottoman Turks, but Britain retained its position as Kuwait's protector. Full sovereignty did not come to Kuwait until 1961.

Kuwait had authorized a British-American company to drill for oil in 1934, but it wasn't until 1946 that the country became a major oil exporter. In 1975, the government nationalized, or took total control of, the oil companies, thus becoming one of the wealthiest countries in the world.

With billions of dollars at its disposal, Kuwait began to improve its schools, roads, and hospitals. The country had free primary and secondary education, free health care, and no income tax. While the government sought to modernize the country, it also wanted to remain faithful to its Islamic tradition.

To maintain and secure its wealth, Kuwait has invested heavily in other countries, including the United States. It has also brought thousands of Arabs to work in the country, though mainly in menial jobs. In fact, less than half the 1.9 million people who live in Kuwait are Kuwaiti citizens. Government rules give citizenship only to males who can show Kuwaiti ties for more than 50 years.

Efforts to broaden government rule beyond the emir have so far failed. The emir dissolved a national assembly in 1986, fearing it was undermining his authority.

Relations with Iraq, Kuwait's neighbor to the north, have been shaky for more than a decade. Territorial disputes were frequent. Kuwait, however, built close ties with Saudi Arabia, its neighbor to the south.

Kuwait supported Iraq in its war with Iran from 1980 to 1988. In 1987, during the final months of the Iran-Iraq war, Kuwait asked the Soviet Union and the United States to guard its oil tankers in the Gulf, which had become Iranian targets.

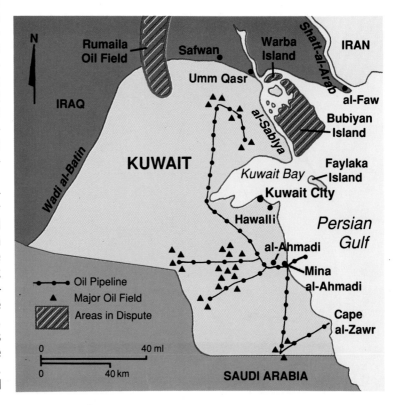

accounted for about 25 percent of the oil used in the United States. Just 20 years later, in 1990, the percentage of foreign oil used in the United States had doubled to more than 50 percent.

As one consequence of low oil prices, the United States failed to develop alternative energy sources. When oil is cheap and plentiful, there is no incentive for businesses to explore new energy sources. But when supplies of oil are scarce, the United States grows vulnerable.

A hundred years ago, no one could have foreseen that one day the countries of the Persian Gulf would possess the wealth and power that they do today. Nearly all the land was—and still is—desert, hostile and uninhabitable. During the summer, temperatures reach 120 degrees, denying life to most living creatures. In the winter months, temperatures fall, but still average about 80 degrees.

The discovery of oil at the turn of the century changed the Gulf forever. The old desert trading posts are now sleek, modern cities with skyscrapers, shopping malls, indoor skating rinks, parks, and universities. For years, foreign oil companies, mostly from the United States and Britain, owned and operated the thousands of oil wells that dot the region. But as Gulf nations gained independence from colonial powers, they took control of the oil wells and oil income. The vast profits from oil have turned many impoverished desert kingdoms into major international economic forces. Many Kuwaitis and Saudis became wealthy beyond anyone's imagination. Much of the money went to modernize the oil-rich nations, but a lot of it was wasted on such luxuries as private jets, mansions, and yachts.

At least that's what many poor Arabs say. Not all Arab countries are favored with oil wealth—in fact, most of the Arab world lives in poverty. Thousands of children die each day in Egypt, Yemen, and Jordan. Arabs without oil resent the wealth of the lucky few. They argue that oil fortunes should help poor and needy Arabs.

OPEC leaders met in Geneva, Switzerland in March 1986 to discuss oil production and pricing for the world market. Seated on the right is the Iraqi minister of oil Qassim Ahmed Taki. Gholamreza Aghazadeh, minister of petroleum for Iran, is about to be seated on the left.

OPEC and the Gulf

In 1960, the major oil producers, except the United States and the Soviet Union, formed the Organization of Petroleum Exporting Countries (OPEC). The group numbers 13 nations, including Iran, Iraq, Saudi Arabia, and Kuwait, but also includes nations from outside the Gulf. The main purpose of OPEC is to control production and keep prices at a profitable level.

In recent years, however, there have been struggles within OPEC on just how much oil to pump. Countries with large reserves, such as Saudi Arabia and Kuwait, usually have pushed for more oil and lower prices. They have argued that high prices would lead major consumers to go back to developing alternative sources of energy, such as solar, wind, or nuclear power. Other OPEC members, with smaller reserves and greater case needs, have called for reduced production and higher prices.

OPEC members meet at least twice a year to set production quotas, or allowances, for each member. Meetings are not always friendly. Some members argue for higher quotas, citing special circumstances. During the Iran-Iraq war, for example, both nations wanted to pump more oil to pay for weapons. Meetings sometimes drag on for days, as oil ministers debate and negotiate.

Even when they reach agreement, there is no guarantee that any OPEC member will not produce more than its quota. OPEC employs a staff to keep an eye on production, but the nations who seek higher production limits often cheat.

In the late 1980s, Iraq pushed hard for high prices. It needed the money to rebuild the damage from its war with Iran and to pay its war debts. But Kuwait and most other Gulf nations were free of debts. They supported high production, which meant low prices. Economically, this policy hurt Iraq. Iraq threatened Kuwait, to force lower oil production. It also claimed that the Kuwaitis were pumping more than their fair share of oil from the Rumaila oil field, an oil source that flows beneath the Iraqi and Kuwaiti border. Iraq also claimed the right to two Kuwaiti islands—Bubiyan and Warba—and demanded to have its war debts to Kuwait forgiven. Saddam Hussein argued that his leadership position in the Middle East, as well as Iraq's war with Iran, benefited Kuwait.

Chapter 3

The Birthplace of Western Civilization

Iraq's history is rich and ancient. Many historians believe it is where Western civilization began thousands of years ago. The first people known to have lived in the land called Mesopotamia were the Sumerians. They are credited with developing the world's first system of writing.

After the Sumerians, the Babylonians and Assyrians came to live in the fertile river valleys near the Tigris and Euphrates rivers. The Babylonians were known for their scientific accomplishments. Their astronomers developed the system of measuring time that we still use today. The Assyrians are best remembered for their strong military skills, especially for establishing the first professional army.

After the Arab conquest of Iraq in the 7th century A.D., the country served as the power center of the Abbasids, the longest-lived of the Muslim ruling dynasties. During much of this period, Baghdad was an important center of literature and art. Works of philosophy, mathematics, geography, and astronomy also flourished in Iraq during this era.

Baghdad was captured in 1258 by the Mongol Hulagu. During this time, the great canals of Mesopotamia were destroyed, marking the beginning of the end of the culture that had previously thrived. The Ottoman Turks conquered the region in the 1500s. Almost 400 years of rule by the Ottomans followed—a chaotic time filled with tribal disputes, raids from the desert, and a war with Iran.

With a noble but often brutal past, Iraq has seen turmoil for centuries

Opposite:
A stone tablet from 12th-century Mesopotamia that shows an eagle goddess harvesting fruit. Mesopotamia, located where the Tigris and Euphrates rivers meet in southeastern Iraq, is considered to be the birthplace of Western civilization.

Throughout World War I, Iraq gradually became occupied by the British, who removed the Turks from power in that country. The British installed a provisional wartime government. After World War I, the British established a civil government in Iraq. That government remained relatively unchallenged until 1920, when tribal rebellions began to arise. It was at this time that the decision was made to create an Iraqi Arab state—one that would eventu-

In 1979, Iraq's President Ahmed Hassan al-Bakr (left) resigned from office under great threat. The man who unseated him was then vice-chairman of Iraq's Revolutionary Command Council, Saddam Hussein (right).

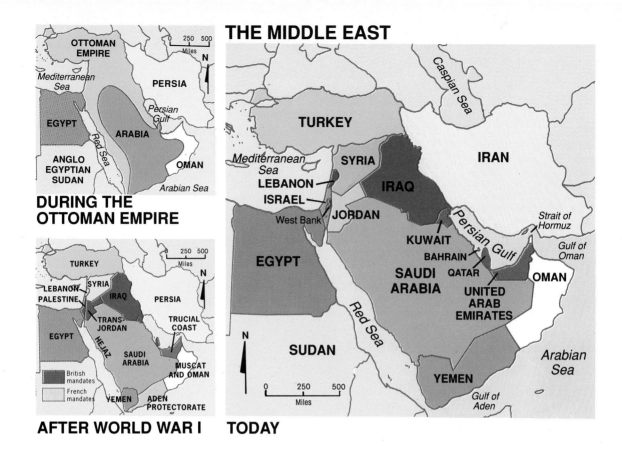

THE MIDDLE EAST

DURING THE OTTOMAN EMPIRE

AFTER WORLD WAR I

TODAY

Colonialism in the Middle East

The French and British drew up the borders of the Arab countries in the Middle East after World War I in 1918. The Ottoman Empire, which ruled much of the Arab world for 400 years, had sided with the defeated Germany and lost its large land holdings in the Persian Gulf.

The League of Nations, forerunner of the United Nations, gave France and Britain the authority to carve up much of the Middle East around 1920. Both countries already had a string of colonies that stretched over much of the world. In many cases, the borders that were drawn showed more concern for London and Paris than for the traditions of the native people.

The French set up republics, modeled on France, in Syria and Lebanon. The British created monarchies, modeled on Great Britain, and installed members of the Hashemite family in Jordan and Iraq. The Hashemite family had led a revolt against the Turks.

The British also set up governments in Egypt, central Arabia, and Kuwait. Britain installed traditional rulers with whom it had built close ties during the war.

After World War II in 1945, France and Britain began to cut their ties and grant independence. The war had weakened the European nations. They could no longer control their colonies. In addition, people in the colonies began pushing for independence. They wanted to be free to rule themselves.

By the mid-1960s, nearly all the Middle East was free of the colonial powers. Even so, much of the Arab world remains suspicious of Westerners. They fear that foreign powers, particularly the United States, will try to impose their will on less powerful Arab nations.

ally achieve independence. Britain accepted a mandate from the League of Nations, which provided for the formation of an Iraqi cabinet and the installation of an Iraqi head of state. For the following 12 years, Iraq slowly refined its methods of self-governance and aligned itself for a position in the community of nations. On October 3, 1932, at the end of the mandate period, Iraq was admitted to the League of Nations as an independent state with King Faisal the crowned leader.

The Struggle for Leadership

Early in World War II (1939–1945), British troops returned to Iraq to put down a revolt by native supporters of Nazi Germany, but the British left again at the end of the war.

In the 1950s, as in many Muslim countries, popular revolt broke out against the monarchy. Throughout the Middle East, students and dissidents took to the streets, calling for a greater popular role in government. They denounced rulers for being too aloof from the people and indifferent to their needs, of imitating Western ways, and of taking no pride in Arab history, customs, or culture.

In Iraq, the movement took a distinctive form. In 1958, army officers overthrew the king and declared the country a republic. To emphasize their desire for change, the new rulers reversed the king's pro-Western policies and accepted aid from communist nations. But factions arose among the new leaders of Iraq and, in 1963, a group of army officers from the Baath party seized control.

The Baathists, formally members of the Iraqi Arab Socialist Union, were strict nationalists who favored the promotion of Arab culture. They were also strict enemies of Israel and, later, of Iran.

The Baath party was soon ejected from power, but its members seized the government again in 1968. They have ruthlessly maintained control ever since.

Boys as young as 12 years old have been known to take up arms in the Iraqi militia. Here, youngsters wave AK–47 assault rifles during a training session in Baghdad.

The Baathists stayed in power by brutally suppressing any dissidents or political opponents. Saddam Hussein began his career as the government's chief torturer and climbed over all rivals to reach the top. In 1979, he forced out his superior and became president.

For the vast majority of Iraqis, who take no part in politics, life improved under the Baathists and Saddam. As the country developed its oil resources and grew richer, the government spent money on roads, housing, schools, and hospitals.

The modern Iraq, with a population of 18 million, is about the size of California. More than 50 percent of the

population are Shiite Muslims and 20 percent are Sunni Muslims. The Kurds constitute 20 percent and are the largest non-Arab group in Iraq. About 3 million people live in Baghdad, the capital.

War between Iraq and Iran

Early in 1979, after a bloody revolution, the people in Iraq's neighboring country, Iran, deposed Shah Mohammed Reza Pahlavi.

The new ruler, Ayatollah Ruhollah Khomeini, a Shiite Muslim cleric, opposed the Western ways that had become popular under the shah. He enforced a return to strict Islamic traditions. New laws required women to cover their faces with veils and give up Western dress. Coed swimming was banned, as was the sale of alcohol. Khomeini and the other Muslim leaders forbade Western music, comparing it to the drug opium.

This resurgence of religious fervor frightened many Arab leaders, especially in such neighboring nations as Iraq, Kuwait, and Saudi Arabia. They had tried to strike a balance between modernizing their countries and observing Islam. They built new roads and schools, acquired technical skills, while still holding onto Islamic traditions and ways. Now, they feared that the radical beliefs of Khomeini would spread and topple them from power.

With Iran in turmoil, Saddam saw an opportunity to settle an old score. For years Iran and Iraq had squabbled over control of the Shatt al-Arab waterway between the two countries. It is one of Iraq's few outlets to the Persian Gulf.

In September 1980, Iraq attacked Iran, launching the bloodiest war the Middle East had seen. Iran's fierce resistance surprised Iraq. Saddam expected that if he struck quickly and forcefully, victory would be assured. But instead, the war turned into a bloody stalemate. Neither country gained much territory. Missiles struck Baghdad and other cities. Iraq used chemical weapons, which were

Opposite:
Angry Iranians carry the coffins of victims killed in bombings of Tehran during the Iran-Iraq war. The war lasted for eight years and killed hundreds of thousands of people from both countries.

Saddam Hussein

Saddam Hussein was born to a poor peasant family in 1937. After escaping that impoverished background, he never let anyone get in his way as he clawed his way to power in Iraq. He killed or pushed aside anyone—including members of his family—who posed threats, real or imagined, to that quest.

He grew up in Tikrit, a poor town without electricity or running water, about 100 miles from Baghdad. Saddam's education was haphazard. He left school to become active in politics, and didn't finish high school until he was 24 years old. At that time he was living in Egypt, after fleeing possible arrest in Iraq because of his involvement in an assassination attempt against a political rival.

He returned to Iraq in 1963, already a member of the ruling Baath party. He took the job of state torturer. According to several witnesses, he viciously beat and killed prisoners accused of plotting to overthrow the Baath government.

From then on, except for a brief stay in jail, he steadily rose to the top levels of the Baath party. By the age of 32, he held the second most powerful job in Iraq.

In 1979, he became president, after pressuring his predecessor from office. He quickly sought to strengthen his grip on power, executing many former colleagues. Saddam may have personally killed 20 high-ranking military officers. Like other dicta-

tors, he ordered the killings because he feared those men might seek to undermine his power.

Despite his ruthless ways, many Iraqis admired Saddam. They saw him as a strong leader who had bravely faced up to Western powers. They believed him when he said that he sought to be the defender of the Arab people against foreigners.

They also respected him for building Iraq into a military nation. Saddam spent billions of dollars on the newest weapons and on

trying to develop nuclear arms. At the same time, he built schools, hospitals, and roads.

As Saddam's power grew, his image came to dominate much of Iraq. Huge pictures of him were hung in schools, offices, and on billboards. The evening newscast became almost entirely centered on Saddam's daily activities, no matter how trivial. All of this reminded Iraqis that Saddam was in absolute control, and it served to scare anyone who might think of challenging his authority.

A mural portrait of Saddam Hussein that depicts him as a military hero.

outlawed as inhumane after World War I. The war dragged on for eight years, with both sides ending up as losers. Iran sent children as young as 12 to fight. As Muslims, they believed that if they died fighting, they would become martyrs (holy sufferers) and go to heaven.

The key Iraqi port of Basra on the Shatt al-Arab waterway was caught in the fighting. This seriously hampered Iraq's oil exports and trade with other countries.

Finally, in August 1988, both sides reluctantly agreed to a cease-fire. The actual number of Iraqis killed in the war may never be known. Experts estimate the fighting killed hundreds of thousands. In most countries such an enormous loss of life without a clear victory would mean the ouster of the leader. But Saddam escaped this.

During the next two years, he shrewdly turned up the heat on Kuwait and Saudi Arabia, claiming that Iraq had fought the war to protect them from the radicals in Iran. He demanded that they help pay Iraq's huge war debt.

He also rekindled an old argument with Kuwait over their border and the ownership of several major oil fields. All this distracted the Iraqi people from focusing on Saddam' military failure against Iran.

Saudi Arabia sought to mediate the dispute between Iraq and Kuwait. The two sides even met in Jidda, Saudi Arabia, a day before the August 2 invasion.

No one knows for sure what happened at the meeting. The Iraqis said the Kuwaitis were arrogant and uncompromising. The Kuwaitis said the Iraqis came without any intention of negotiating—probably because Saddam had already decided to invade. In any case, the talks never got off the ground. The Iraqi negotiators left, claiming they needed to talk with important officials in Baghdad. Less than 12 hours later Iraq invaded.

Chapter 4

The U.S. and the U.N. Take Action

O nce it became obvious that Saddam wasn't going to quickly withdraw his troops from Kuwait, the nations opposed to the invasion sought tougher action by the Security Council of the United Nations. The council had already condemned and criticized Iraq for the invasion, but these nations now wanted more.

The nations that had lined up against Saddam met to discuss the best course of action to press for a withdrawal. They quickly rejected any idea of a swift military attack. For one thing, their forces were not ready to fight.

After a day or two, the nations agreed to ban trade with Iraq. Such a ban is a kind of economic sanction. Sanctions hurt a country in its pocketbook. If no one will trade with a nation, it cannot earn much money. This would not matter that much to a self-sufficient country, with its own farms and industry. But Iraq buys most of its food and manufactured goods from other nations. The goal was to strangle Iraq economically and to force its withdrawal from Kuwait with no lives lost.

The Security Council quickly passed tough economic sanctions. Of the 15 members, only two nations abstained, or refused to vote. The council had rarely seen such unity.

Nearly all nations quickly cut off trade with Iraq. No one would sell products to Iraq; no one would buy its products.

The first large group of U.S. troops for "Desert Shield" were sent to Saudi Arabia at the request of King Fahd

Opposite:
A catapult officer gives the "all clear" to the pilot of an F-14 Tomcat, about to take off from the decks of the USS *Independence* stationed in the Persian Gulf.

The final vote to impose sanctions against Iraq was taken by the United Nations Security Council on August 6, 1990. Of the 15 members on the council, only Cuba and Yemen abstained from the voting.

For instance, Iraq couldn't buy wheat from the United States or machinery from France, as it had before the sanctions.

The sanctions also made it impossible for Iraq to sell its oil. Iraq depends on oil sales for nearly all its wealth. Without that money, Iraq faced a cash squeeze.

To help make the sanctions work, the United States and other nations halted ships leaving or going to Iraq. Warships turned back those carrying banned products. At first, Saddam ordered his oil tankers to sneak around the blockade. But the multinational force had sophisticated radar that easily tracked down the Iraqi vessels. Within a few days Saddam ordered the tankers to stay in port.

In Washington, President Bush launched Operation Desert Shield. He rushed the first large group of U.S. troops at the request of King Fahd of Saudi Arabia. Iraqi

The effect of economic sanctions and embargoes against Iraq was quickly seen on the streets of Baghdad, where citizens stood in line for hours to obtain bread rations.

troops were on the border, and King Fahd feared an invasion. Troops poured in by air and sea. Other nations, including France, Britain, Egypt, Morocco, and Syria, also sent forces. But the great majority of the troops in the desert were from the United States.

Iraq Tightens Its Grip

In Kuwait, the situation grew uglier and bloodier. Iraqi troops in the capital looted and plundered the city of all its valuables. They stripped department stores of their goods. They robbed hospitals of equipment and banks of money and gold. They shipped any object of value to Iraq.

Those Kuwaitis who were fortunate, fled. They packed all they could and left for Saudi Arabia. They crossed the desert at night by car or camel or on foot. Iraqi soldiers captured and killed many of them.

In Baghdad, Saddam announced that Kuwait was no longer an independent country but a part of Iraq—its 19th province or state. All Kuwaitis were Iraqi citizens, he said, and he was their ruler.

He also ordered all foreign embassies in Kuwait closed. Embassies represent a country's interests in a foreign nation. Saddam said to keep an embassy open in Kuwait was "an act of aggression." Since Kuwait no longer existed, he said, they were not needed.

The U.S. Embassy and a few others in Kuwait City refused to close. The ambassadors believed that if they followed Saddam's order, it would show acceptance of his actions and agreement with his claims. In addition, the ambassadors said their countrymen who were stuck in Kuwait needed their help.

Saddam Seizes "Human Shields"

Saddam backed up his order by sending troops to surround the embassies, and by cutting off electricity and running water to them. His troops did not, however, invade the

The United Nations Gains World Importance

The bitter rivalry between the United States and the Soviet Union (known as the Cold War) has in the past discouraged either from turning to the United Nations to gain international support. But in 1990, with the Cold War at an end, President Bush eagerly sought the help of the U.N. in his stand against Iraq. He repeatedly stressed that it was not just the United States but the entire international community against Iraq. Indeed, the U.N. Security Council condemned the invasion less than 24 hours after Iraqi troops crossed the Kuwaiti border.

The U.N. was created in 1945, at the end of World War II, to help bring and keep peace in the world. Fifty nations signed the charter establishing it, and the organization has now grown to 159 nations.

Six major organs make up the U.N. They are the General Assembly, the Security Council, the Secretariat, the Economic and Social Council, the International Court of Justice, and the Trusteeship Council.

The General Assembly is the only major organ in which all members are represented. Each nation has one vote. The assembly usually meets for three months a year at U.N. headquarters in New York. The assembly is like a town meeting, in which members can discuss issues that concern them.

The Security Council has the responsibility for keeping peace.

The council has 15 members, five of which are permanent. The permanent members are Britain, China, France, the Soviet Union, and the United States. The General Assembly elects the other ten members to two-year terms.

Each of the five permanent members has the power to veto, or defeat, any important measure.

The permanent members were originally given veto power because they were principal allies in World War II. But the veto power has blocked the Security Council from tackling a number of tough issues. The Soviet Union holds the record for using its veto: In all, it has vetoed more than 100 resolutions.

The Secretariat building of the United Nations

embassies. The U.S. ambassador and his small staff gathered what food they could find and bolted the gate of the embassy. Since there was no running water, they used the embassy swimming pool to keep clean. They kept in touch with Washington by telephone.

The Iraqi president's next action was meant to frighten the United States and its allies. Thousands of foreigners, including many Americans and Europeans, worked in the

The port of Aqaba, in Jordan, was eventually blocked by the U.N. economic sanctions. It had been a key entry point for goods going to Iraq.

Saddam Hussein made a public display of British schoolboy Stuart Lockwood, who was being held hostage in Iraq following the invasion of Kuwait. On a broadcast beamed all over the world, Saddam patted the boy with "fatherly concern" to show how hostages were being treated.

oil industry and other businesses in Iraq and Kuwait. The invasion caught most of these people by surprise, before they could get away from the danger and go back home.

Saddam's response to the sending of U.S. troops to Saudi Arabia was to take many American, Japanese, British, French, Italian, and Irish foreigners hostage. Some foreigners hid in basements. Friendly Kuwaitis gave them help. A few escaped to Saudi Arabia. But many were captured by Iraq.

Saddam sent many of the hostages to important Iraqi military bases, dams, and factories to act as "human

Shifting Alliances in the Arab World

Syria, an Arab nation, is on a U.S. government list of states that support terrorism—the use of violence against innocent victims for a political cause. The United States has often criticized Syria for its aid to terrorists. It has urged Syria to end its support, and has punished it by cutting political contact and financial aid.

But U.S.-Syrian relations changed when Iraq invaded Kuwait. Then, Syria and the United States became allies, teaming up to force Iraq from Kuwait. Syria's President Hafez al-Assad ordered more than 5,000 troops to Saudi Arabia to join the multinational force. President Bush even met with the Syrian president before returning from a Thanksgiving visit to Saudi Arabia.

A soldier from Saudi Arabia's frontier forces stands guard at the border crossing from|Kuwait after Iraq's invasion.

The invasion dramatically shifted the alliances or ties in the Arab world. It also showed that unity in the Arab world was much weaker than the impression Arab leaders tried to give. Before the invasion, Arab leaders said they were united, with few differences among them. The invasion showed otherwise.

What united Arab leaders for more than 40 years was opposition to the state of Israel. Since its creation in 1948, the existence of the Jewish state has angered its Arab neighbors. They argue that the land belongs to the Palestinians and not the Israelis.

Israel and its Arab neighbors have fought four wars. Each time the Arab world has united against Israel. But Israel survives. Many Arab leaders have argued that Israel is the only serious problem in the Middle East.

But the invasion of Kuwait showed that disputes exist in the Arab world. While Saudi Arabia, Egypt, Syria, the United Arab Emirates, and Oman joined with the United States to oppose Iraq, Yemen backed Iraq. The Palestine Liberation Organization also supported Iraq. Eventually, so did Jordan.

President Bush asked Israel to stay on the sidelines. The United States feared that if Israel became involved, the multinational alliance would crumble because Arab nations would resist joining forces with their longtime foe.

shields." Iraq believed that the multinational force would be reluctant to attack these places if it meant killing their own people. Saddam said he would release the hostages if the United States pulled its troops out of the Gulf region. Bush rejected his demand.

The Iraqi leader even went on television with some foreign children and patted one of them on the head. He tried to show that he cared about them. His actions outraged many people.

Saddam did allow, however, tens of thousands of non-Western refugees, a large number of them Egyptians, to leave Iraq. Thousands of people quickly packed their belongings and headed for the border with Jordan. Some left by car, many went by foot.

Jordan was unprepared for the thousands of new arrivals. The government set up camps for the refugees, who waited for ships to go home, but the camps soon became crowded. To ease the crush, ferry service between Jordan and Egypt was increased.

To win broader support, Saddam attempted to link the Kuwait invasion to the issue of the Palestinians. He said he launched the attack on Kuwait to get the world to pay attention to the Palestinian Arabs and their quest for statehood. This call had wide support among many Arabs. They view Israel as the enemy, and they resent the close relations between Israel and the United States.

Thus, Saddam sought to present the crisis not as Iraq against Kuwait, but as Iraq against the United States. The Iraqi leader knew that he could draw support from fellow Arab nations if he placed Israel in the center of the conflict. He was no longer solely fighting for Kuwait but to bring the Palestinian issue to the world's attention. As tensions mounted and impatience grew, Saddam repeatedly threatened to strike Israel first. Saddam knew that such a claim might weaken the bonds between the United States and some of the alliance members, particularly those who were bitter foes of Israel.

Chapter 5

Desert Shield Becomes Desert Storm

Presidential Bush took a bold step in November 1990. He doubled the number of U.S. troops in the Gulf region to more than 400,000. The president said he sent more troops to insure that the multinational force had "an adequate offensive military option."

Those few words from the president signaled a dramatic change. They showed how far the United States was willing to go to get Iraq out of Kuwait. Until November, the president and other leaders said Operation Desert Shield's mission was to protect Saudi Arabia from attack.

The president sent about three army divisions (a division has about 18,000 soldiers) to Saudi Arabia. Most of these were tank units transferred from Western Europe. He also sent 40,000 more marines and three additional aircraft carrier battle groups to join the three carriers already in the Persian Gulf.

The more than 400,000 troops in Saudi Arabia represented about 25 percent of all the men and women in the U.S. armed forces. Although women can't serve in combat, about 230,000 women wear a military uniform. The Defense Department wouldn't give the number of women in the Gulf, but their number was estimated at 15,000.

An estimated 30 percent of the U.S. troops in the Gulf were minorities, with blacks making up the largest single minority group.

U.N. resolution 678 set January 15 as the deadline for Iraqi withdrawal from Kuwait

Opposite:
A U.S. marine awaits instruction under his camouflaged gun post in the sand.

Reporters crowd around members of Congress as they comment on the debate over sanctions instead of war against Iraq. Speaker of the House Thomas Foley is in the center at the microphone, Senate Majority Leader George Mitchell is at Foley's left, and House Majority Leader Richard Gephardt—who was among the most vocal advocates of sanctions in the Congressional debates—is behind Mitchell.

This military buildup was one of the largest since World War II. The Defense Department said that soon, more than a third of all its forces would be in the Gulf, and two-thirds of the Marine Corps was already there.

The president's decision was underscored by the fact that non-regular, part-time servicemen and women were also involved. Reserve and National Guard combat units were placed on active duty. Those soldiers normally work at regular jobs during the week and serve in the military on weekends and during the summer. They include doctors, pilots, teachers, and police officers.

Some Americans were upset at the president's plan. They doubted the president's wisdom in sending so many troops

Who Can Declare War

The Capitol

President Bush wasn't the first commander in chief of the U.S. armed forces to battle Congress on whether he needed its approval to wage war.

In fact, Thomas Jefferson was the first to fight a war without seeking approval from Congress. He sent the Navy to whip the Barbary pirates in the early 1800s.

Members of Congress and others argue that the U.S. Constitution, which outlines the separation of powers among the three branches of government, gives Congress the sole authority to declare war. They point to Article 1, Section 8. It says, "The Congress shall have Power ... to declare War." They argue that the framers of the Constitution purposely gave Congress this power because it was too awesome a responsibility for one person.

Congress has only declared war five times—most recently in 1941, after the Japanese attacked Pearl Harbor. Yet the United States has been involved in an estimated 130 military actions. The most recent commitment of troops before Saudi Arabia was in 1989, when U.S. troops invaded Panama. The United States then brought President Manuel Noriega to Florida, and planned to put him on trial for drug trafficking charges.

Those who argue that the president doesn't need congressional permission to commit American forces to combat also use the Constitution to back their case.

They cite Article 2, Section 2. It says, "The President shall be Commander in Chief of the Army and Navy of the United States." They add that seeking congressional support would hamper the president's flexibility, giving an edge to an opponent. They also argue that a national debate might undermine unity.

In the past, Congress has usually supported any president's military actions. And since Congress controls the purse strings of the nation's budget, the president cannot long wage a war that Congress does not approve.

The White House

STANDARD ISSUE

This female marine arrives in Saudi Arabia dressed for desert duty.

Day uniform, sun hat, and neckerchief

M-16 rifle with sling, 30-round magazine
Total weight: 8.76 pounds

Fragmentation vest
Total weight: 9 pounds

Suspenders for hanging equipment
Total weight: 3.5 pounds

Chemical protection overgarment, gloves, inserts for gloves, overshoes, atropine kit (antidote for nerve gas), chemical detection kit

Helmet, helmet cover and goggles, pistol and case

Personal items that include: insect spray, suntan lotion, water purification tablets, foot powder, lip balm, first-aid kit

In addition:
Large field pack
Sleeping bag
Digging tool
Rations (includes canned food or freeze-dried food, rolled bread, fresh fruit)
Night parka liner (for cold desert nights)
Body armor cover
2-quart water canteens
Night trousers for sleeping in the desert

Hot-weather boots
Total weight: 3.8 pounds

SHOPPING LIST FOR DESERT SHIELD	
MEDICAL SUPPLIES	
Sunscreen, 150,000 bottles	$219,000
Lip balm, 6,000 boxes @100 tubes	99,000
Foot powder, 230,000 tubes	80,000
Chigger repellent, 40,000 cans	76,400
FOOD SUPPLIES	
Hamburger, 2,000,000 pounds	$2,000,000
Fresh fruit and vegetables, 2,000 pounds	N/A
CLOTHING	
Chemical protection suits, 168,000	$68.15 each
Goggles, 100,000+	3.85 each
Sewing kits, 100,000+	3-5 each

to Saudi Arabia. They argued that it was too soon for military action against Iraq. They said that if the economic sanctions were given enough time—a year or so—they might very well work. But the president and others said that only military force would push Iraq from Kuwait. They argued that Saddam was a dictator who would let thousands of his own people die to keep Kuwait.

Others complained that Kuwait wasn't worth dying for. They argued that Kuwait is an undemocratic nation ruled by a feudal monarch. What's more, the huge price tag for Operation Desert Shield angered many Americans. Just the first five months of the operation cost $10 billion. The estimate for 1991 was $30 billion. Other nations, particularly Kuwait and Saudi Arabia, promised to pay most of the cost. Even so, despite increased oil revenues for Saudi Arabia and other Gulf nations, the United States was footing much of the bill.

Problems in the Sand

Nature provided the two biggest problems U.S. troops faced in the deserts of Saudi Arabia—sand and heat. As you'd expect in a desert, sand is everywhere. It is so fine that it gets into everything.

Although that's annoying for a soldier, it can easily create havoc for military equipment, such as guns, trucks, and even tanks. Sand can clog rifles and engines, making them useless. Soldiers spent hours keeping their equipment clean and free of sand.

The sun can kill. Temperatures push 120 degrees during the summer, and soldiers must drink five gallons of water a day to stay healthy. If they don't, they can quickly become dehydrated. One major challenge the U.S. military command faced was how to get water to troops in the field. A few oases with drinkable water dot the desert but not enough for an army. To quench soldiers' thirst, the U.S. Army brought in scores of tanker trucks to deliver water.

Besides the sand and heat, there is the problem of knowing where you are. Getting lost in the desert is easy. Soldiers can't depend on road signs or natural landmarks to find their way. Everything looks the same.

Fortunately, U.S. troops in the desert often carry sophisticated electronic compasses. These devices are able to tell soldiers their exact location. Like many Iraqi troops, U.S. forces trained in the desert, and know how to get around and survive.

Adjusting to the sizzling weather wasn't the only change for soldiers. Saudi Arabia is a very closed society that strictly follows Islam. It even forbids the practice of any other religion. Women have very few rights.

At Christmas, which is a Chris-tian and not an Islamic holiday, U.S. troops held religious services but out of the sight of the press to avoid offending the Saudis. Even comedian Bob Hope toned down his traditional Christmas show for the troops.

Military commanders told U.S. forces to stay out of trouble. They reminded them that the Saudis are sensitive and frown on many social activities that Westerners take for granted. For instance, in Saudi Arabia men and women can't dance together. Saudi women wear dark robes and cover their faces with veils. Alcoholic beverages are strictly prohibited.

Back home, many Americans were upset about the restrictions. They argued that the U.S. military was too concerned about Saudi sensitivities and not enough about the needs of U.S. servicemen and women who were risking their lives.

An M-1 tank from the United States Army bursts through a sandy tank trap.

What's more, some members of Congress were concerned that their branch of government wouldn't be consulted in the decision on whether the United States should go to war. They said the U.S. Constitution gives Congress clear final authority to declare war.

They also said the president and his advisers had not explained clearly the reasons why the United States should go to war. Some questioned whether the nation's vital interests were at stake. They also pointed out that the president's stated reasons and goals had changed several times in the months after the invasion.

President Bush first said the U.S. troops were in Saudi Arabia to protect "our way of life." He warned that if Saddam controlled the oil of Kuwait, the world's economy would be in danger.

But later the president said that U.S. actions were not based on oil, but on democratic principles and resistance to aggression. On Thanksgiving Day, while visiting troops in Saudi Arabia, President Bush presented another reason for confrontation. He said he wanted to prevent Iraq from acquiring nuclear weapons, the most deadly of all weapons.

Iraq had spent many millions on developing nuclear weapons. Experts were divided on how long it would take before Saddam had such weapons. Some said one year, others estimated ten years. The president believed now was the time to take action.

"Every day that passes brings Saddam one step closer to realizing his goal of a nuclear weapons arsenal," the president said. He added that Iraq had to be stopped before it got such weapons, and warned that otherwise Saddam would blackmail other tiny neighbors.

But the president was only willing to take action if the international community supported the United States. Just days after he returned from Saudi Arabia, he got his wish. The U.N. Security Council voted 12-2 to authorize the use of force to get Iraq out of Kuwait. (Cuba and Yemen were the two nations to vote against the resolution, and China abstained.)

U.S. General Colin L. Powell, chairman of the Joint Chiefs of Staff, was responsible for coordinating all communication between Washington and Saudi Arabia during the war in the Gulf.

U.S. Secretary of State James Baker shakes hands with Iraqi Foreign Minister Tariq Aziz in Geneva, Switzerland on January 9, 1991. Their talks did not prevent the war.

U.N. resolution 678 set January 15 as the deadline for an Iraqi withdrawal. It gave the multinational forces power "to use all the means necessary" to evict Iraq. Soviet Foreign Secretary Eduard Shevardnadze, who strongly supported the resolution, said the January 15 deadline gave Iraq "one last chance."

Many called the resolution historic. They said it was bold and daring. The council had authorized the use of force only once before. That was in 1950, for the Korean War.

In Baghdad, Saddam rejected the resolution. He vowed that he would keep Kuwait even if war was necessary. He warned that thousands of American soldiers would die in the sands of the Kuwaiti deserts.

The Iraqi leader's words were harsh, but he took another action that surprised many. Saddam announced that he would let all the remaining foreign hostages go home. The

Opposite:
Troops in Nuclear-Biological-Chemical (NBC) suits take a water break to prevent dehydration in the blazing temperatures of the desert.

news of the release brought tears and smiles to hundreds of families in the United States and other nations.

The United States arranged for flights to pick up the few hundred Americans in Kuwait who had eluded the Iraqis. The U.S. ambassador and his small staff ate one last can of tuna fish and headed home. The "human shield" hostages were taken to Baghdad and put on planes for home.

For a moment it looked as if a peaceful settlement might be worked out. The return of the hostages was a gesture of peace. The United States and Iraq said they would meet to discuss peace. But they couldn't agree on a date.

New hope for avoiding war came with the announcement of a meeting between Secretary of State James Baker and Iraqi Foreign Minister Tariq Aziz, scheduled for January 9 in Geneva. After six hours of talks, however, the world was no closer to avoiding a war in the Persian Gulf. Both sides seemed unwilling to compromise on their demands.

The Final Stretch for Peace

Right up to the last moment, diplomats tried to initiate a peace plan. Just three days before the January 15 deadline, for instance, U.N. Secretary-General Javier Perez de Cuellar flew to Baghdad in a last-ditch effort to avoid war. But his mission failed. He met with Saddam, but the Iraqi president was unwilling to budge. He refused offers for further negotiations and was determined not to withdraw from Kuwait.

Then, the 15th came. Even at that late date there was still hope that Saddam would yield.

The tense wait ended just before 3 A.M. (Iraqi time) on Thursday, January 17, when U.S. and allied forces struck at targets in Iraq and Kuwait. That morning Operation Desert Shield had become Operation Desert Storm.

Many Americans learned of the attacks from television news. Correspondents in Baghdad, looking out of their hotel rooms, vividly described the air raid. The Iraqi capital was aglow with anti-aircraft fire and explosions.

General H. Norman Schwarzkopf was the commander of all U.S. forces in the Middle East during the war against Iraq.

HIGH-TECH WEAPONRY

PATRIOT MISSILES
COST: $123 million
FUNCTION: To protect ground facilities by intercepting enemy aircraft and missiles.
DISTINCTION: During the opening days of the war, Patriot missiles prevented numerous attacks on Saudi Arabia and Israel by destroying Scud missiles in mid-air.

STEALTH FIGHTER
COST: $106 million
FUNCTION: To accomplish long-range precision bombing by flying extremely low to the ground undetected by enemy radar.
DISTINCTION: Stealth bombers were among the first aircraft to hit Iraqi command-and-control centers, dealing Saddam Hussein's army a crucial blow early in the war.

APACHE HELICOPTER
COST: $32 million
FUNCTION: Employs rockets, "hellfire" anti-armor missiles, and sophisticated computer technology that can seek out and destroy tanks during the day or night.
DISTINCTION: From the air, Apaches can deliver powerful destruction to artillery targets on the ground, giving the allied forces a fighting edge in a ground-based war.

TOW ANTI-TANK MISSILES
COST: Varies widely
FUNCTION: Mounted on the roofs of allied HUMVEES (all-terrain vehicles), TOW missiles can destroy enemy tanks and drive quickly out of danger, before their shots are answered.
DISTINCTION: Used as an effective close-range weapon in ground fighting, capable of great mobility in the sand.

NIGHT-VISION GOGGLES
COST: $200,000 to equip each fighter bomber
FUNCTION: To amplify starlight by 25,000 times for aircraft pilots, tank drivers, and infantry who undertake missions at night and attack at low altitudes without using radar that can be detected by the enemy.
DISTINCTION: Night-vision goggles enabled soldiers to see clearly up to seven miles in complete darkness. Fighter bomber pilots who wore the goggles achieved great bombing accuracy with night bombing raids.

War!

"The liberation
of Kuwait
has begun."
–George Bush,
Jan. 17, 1991

The Iraqi capital city of
Baghdad fell under siege in
the early morning hours of
January 17, 1991, when
allied forces began the air
attacks that started the war.

Later that evening, President Bush addressed the nation, explaining why the United States and its coalition partners had gone to war. He said, "Our goal is not the conquest of Iraq. It is the liberation of Kuwait."

Early Successes and Guarded Reactions

U.S. military experts called the first day successful, but they warned citizens not to become too confident. The allied attacks had gone as planned, knocking out much of Iraq's air force and missile sites. Only one U.S. plane had been downed by the Iraqis, and the pilot was listed as missing in action.

The next morning Saddam appeared in public, defiant. His government vowed to force the allies into "the mud of defeat and surrender."

Despite his earlier vows, Saddam had not yet targeted Israel. But during the early morning on the second day, Iraq fired Scud missiles at the Jewish state. (Scuds are long-range missiles that can be launched from mobile missile launchers as well as stationary ones.) At least seven missiles hit Israel in the first attack, most near Tel Aviv, but only a few people were injured.

The United States urged Israel not to retaliate, fearing that an Israeli raid on Iraq would cause Arab nations to pull out of the anti-Saddam coalition and align in a war against the Jewish state.

The Iraqis launched similar missile attacks on Saudi Arabia, but U.S. Patriot "anti-missile" missiles knocked out the Iraqi Scuds seconds before they hit their intended targets. The Patriots, which were later sent to Israel, became the technological stars of the opening days of the war.

Waging War on the Environment

The war soon also became an environmental danger. During the week of January 21, Iraq began pouring millions of gallons of oil from Kuwaiti oilfields into the Persian Gulf.

Experts estimated the intentional oilspill to be more than a dozen times larger than the massive 1989 spill in Alaska.

As the war raged on, new questions arose about the loyalty of Iraqi soldiers to their cause. By January 29, allied forces had captured approximately 105 Iraqi soldiers, many of whom defected or surrendered. Suspicions were raised concerning more than 100 Iraqi warplanes that flew to Iran in the first weeks of the war. Many thought those Iraqi pilots had defected from the war as well. Others speculated that Saddam was taking some of his best weaponry "out of action" to save it for an attack in the future. Most people, however, were baffled about the motivations behind this mysterious move. As he had from the very onset of this crisis, Saddam Hussein would keep the rest of the world guessing indefinitely.

The Fight for Khafji

The first serious test of the allied ground forces came during the second week of the war when Iraqi troops invaded Khafji, a small abandoned Saudi coastal town just ten miles from the Kuwaiti border. More than 2,000 Iraqi soldiers moved into the port town with tanks and armored personnel carriers. Within hours of the Iraqi movements, allied forces responded, led by Saudi and Qatari soldiers. They sought to push the Iraqis back across the border.

The battle for Khafji was fierce. U.S. Marines fired artillery weapons into the town, while Iraqi forces tried to dig in. At one point, Iraqi tanks pointed their turrets to the rear, a sign of surrender, but instead of giving up quickly, turned and fired their guns on the Saudi soldiers.

After 36 hours of fighting, allied forces retook Khafji. Nearly 500 Iraqi soldiers were taken prisoner and more than 20 Iraqi tanks were destroyed.

In the fighting for Khafji, a female U.S. soldier was believed to have been taken prisoner, the first time a woman serving as a soldier had been officially listed in wartime as missing in action. Although women are not allowed to serve in combat roles, many are assigned to units that bring them close to the fighting.

The U.S. military reported that 11 marines died in the battle for Khafji, but seven of those were mistakenly killed by a U.S. missile, or "friendly fire."

Meanwhile, allied forces continued their daily aerial pounding of Iraq. The allies said they controlled the skies, despite the occasional loss of a plane to Iraqi anti-aircraft fire. The allied forces also said that the Iraqi navy had been eliminated as a threat. Although small, Iraq's navy was considered dangerous. Several Iraqi naval vessels sought to escape to Iran.

From Baghdad, throughout all of this, Saddam remained determined to continue the fight and was confident of victory. In an interview with Peter Arnett of Cable News Network, the Iraqi leader discounted allied successes. "You see," he said, "they were defeated, they were dealt a defeat, the moment they signed the decision to launch the aggression, because they have signed a wrong, unjust decision."

During the week of February 11, Chairman of the Joint Chiefs of Staff Colin Powell and Defense Secretary Richard Cheney traveled to Saudi Arabia. Their mission, as they described it, was to observe firsthand how allied operations were faring. The world knew, however, that Powell and Cheney were going to discuss the strategies for the impending ground war. After talks with General Schwarzkopf and other military personnel, Powell and Cheney returned to the United States smiling, confident, and not saying much.

Meanwhile, allied air assaults continued to devastate Iraq. As more and more targets and artillery were destroyed, the resolve of the Iraqi troops began to soften. In addition to enduring weeks of constant attack from the air, Iraqi soldiers were living on meager rations, little sleep, and dwindling morale. Supply lines had been cut for weeks. No food or materials were coming through. Iraqi communication systems were nearly all destroyed. There was no way for Baghdad commanders to tell their troops what to do. The Iraqis were sitting in the dark—literally and figuratively.

By the week of February 18, Iraqi surrenders had accelerated. Allied soldiers were taking hundreds of sick and starving Iraqi soldiers to POW camps each day. Nearly every soldier the allies captured was equipped with something white to use for surrender. Thousands of Iraqi soldiers were carrying little packets of bleach, packets they would use to turn a piece of clothing into a flag of surrender. Once captured, the Iraqi soldiers were grateful to their captors. Many were ecstatic.

As the ground war became increasingly unavoidable, the Soviet Union engineered a plan for peace that would—if adopted—avoid a ground war completely. Soviet leader Mikhail Gorbachev met with Tariq Aziz in Moscow to discuss the details. Aziz then took the proposals back to Saddam Hussein for consideration. Diplomacy at that point, however, was little more than an exercise. When the allies learned the specifics of the Soviet plan, they rejected it without hesitation. Most vocal in the rejection were the United States and Great Britain, though many other allies quietly agreed. The problem with the plan, the allies contended, was that it did not satisfy the longstanding demands that had been placed on Iraq. Most importantly, it did not call for complete compliance of all 12 U.N. resolutions. It also suggested too generous a timeframe for a cease-fire and did not address other points that the allies clearly considered non-negotiable. Even though there was no hope for the plan, the Iraqis publically announced their agreement to it.

The final opportunities for an early cease-fire were now exhausted. It was up to the allies to make the next move.

President Bush and his cabinet decided to give Saddam Hussein until noon (U.S. time) on Saturday, February 23, to pull out of Kuwait. The Saturday deadline approached, but no indications of withdrawal appeared. And new stories of torture and atrocities against Kuwaiti citizens only served to heighten the pressure on the allies to act. On Sunday, February 24, at approximately 4:00 to 6:00 A.M. Iraqi time, allied forces began their assault on the ground.

The 100 Hours

From the very outset, the ground assault went far better than anyone ever anticipated. Although allied commanders knew that Iraqis were essentially fighting "blind," without any tactical communication, they never underestimated the power the Iraqis had in numbers.

The first day on the ground proved the brilliance of General Schwarzkopf's strategy. The assault was based on two key tactics: First, an apparent "build-up" of marines off the eastern shores of Kuwait fooled the Iraqis into thinking the allies were going to land an amphibious assault. In anticipation, Iraq concentrated much of its power in eastern Kuwait. Second, in conjunction with the first tactic, allied forces moved west and then north to surround Iraqi troops. Having all escape routes systematically cut off, the Iraqi troops were forced to fight or surrender. The choice for most Iraqi soldiers took little time to make—they surrendered.

By the second day of the ground war, operations were speeding up. Ground assaults were met with little resistance and allied forces advanced far ahead of their planned schedule. In the midst of this fast-paced victory, however, disaster struck. An Iraqi Scud missile headed for Saudi Arabia broke up in the air and plunged its warhead into an American barracks near Dhahran. The blast killed 28 soldiers and wounded an additional 90. This tragic twist of fate would cause, in a matter of seconds, almost a third of all American battle deaths for the entire war.

From the moment allied forces broke through the Iraqi line, Saddam's soldiers began surrendering in massive numbers. By Tuesday, the allies were holding more than 30,000 POWs. That morning, Kuwaiti citizens awoke to the sound of Iraqi tanks pulling out of Kuwait City. Allied forces were soon to arrive.

Tuesday and Wednesday were filled with allied victories in various tank battles near Kuwait City. Neither the regular troops nor Iraq's elite Republican Guard could put up enough of a fight to stop the momentum of the allied advance. By Wednesday night, February 27, Kuwait City was in allied hands and more than 100,000 Iraqi soldiers had surrendered. The liberation of Kuwait was assured.

Having Kuwait City and other decisive victories firmly in hand, President Bush gathered his cabinet for a strategy session on Wednesday. With their military objectives met, the president's advisors agreed: The war was all but over. Now the final phases were to be put into action.

Around 5:00 A.M. Iraqi time (9:00 P.M. U.S.)—after only 100 hours of ground battle—the shooting officially stopped. President Bush, appearing on television, opened his speech with these words: "Kuwait is liberated. Iraq's army is defeated. Our military objectives are met. Kuwait is once more in the hands of Kuwaitis in control of their own destiny."

A young Kuwaiti girl proudly waves her nation's flag as she passes by a group of American Marines. Celebration filled the streets of Kuwait City on February 27, 1991, only hours after liberation was achieved.

The Final Outcome

The days following the cease-fire were filled with joyous celebrations in Kuwait and around the world. Diplomats went quickly into action, laying the groundwork for a Middle East peace and stability that would last. The balance of power had been greatly changed. Iraq's army, once one of the world's most formidable, was severely weakened. All told, Iraq had suffered loss or damage of an estimated 85 percent of its tanks, 89 percent of its artillery, 49 percent of its aircraft, and more than 100,000 of its soldiers. By contrast, allied forces suffered a total count of 149 killed and 513 wounded during the entire 43 days of the war.

Although the battles were over, many issues remained to be resolved. Kuwait had suffered greatly—before leaving, the Iraqis had set fire to hundreds of oil wells, and smoke from the fires darkened the sky. Iraq, too, had suffered, largely from allied bombing. Saddam Hussein remained in power, but revolts broke out against him and his future was unclear. So was the future of the post-war Middle East and Iraq's role in it.

The Persian Gulf War took a great toll in lives and destruction. And there are still those who question whether the use of force was worth what was achieved. But the war did enable some positive things to happen. The conflict re-established the United Nations as a credible and effective force in world politics. The war also refocused attention on the Palestinian problem and convinced the world of its urgency. And finally, the victory of the allies, led by the Americans, revived a sense of pride in the United States and its military. For the first time in almost 46 years, U.S. soldiers returned home to a hero's welcome and the thanks of a grateful nation. President Bush, in his speech on February 27, 1991, summed up the war. Bush said, "No one country can claim victory as its own. It was not only a victory for Kuwait, but a victory for all the coalition partners. This is a victory for the United Nations, for all mankind, for the rule of law, and for what is right."

Chronology

B.C.

c. 10,000   Prehistoric peoples in Near East begin to harvest grain.

c. 3500   Early Sumerian sketches show first known use of wheel.

c. 3000   Sumerians develop first known written language.

A.D.

750   Abbasid Dynasty begins; Hashimiya in Iraq becomes its capital.

1258   Baghdad is captured by the Mongol Hulagu.

c. 1530–40   Ottomans conquer Persia; Ottoman rule lasts almost 400 years.

1899   Kuwait accepts British protection to avoid Ottoman domination.

1914–18   World War I brings defeat and collapse of the Ottoman Empire.

Britain recognizes Kuwait as independent from Ottoman Turks.

1921   Iraq is established as a kingdom under its first king, Faisal I.

1932   Iraq admitted to League of Nations as independent state.

Saudi Arabia is created.

1939-45   World War II. British regain control in Middle East, then leave region.

United Nations is officially created.

1958   Iraqi army officers overthrow the king and declare the country a republic.

1960   OPEC is founded.

1961   Kuwait gains full sovereignty.

1963   Baath party siezes control of Iraqi government.

1973   OPEC cuts world oil production and causes gas crisis in many nations.

1979   Saddam Hussein pushes President Ahmed Hassan al-Bakr from power and assumes control of Iraq's government.

OPEC cuts world supply of oil to raise prices; gas crisis in United States.

1980-88   Iran–Iraq War devastates both countries, kills hundreds of thousands, and ends in a stalemate.

1990   **August 2:** Iraqi tanks roll into Kuwait City; Iraqi occupation of Kuwait begins.

August 6: U.N. Security Council votes to impose sanctions on Iraq.

November: U.N. resolution 678 sets January 15 as deadline for Iraqi withdrawal and authorizes use of force if deadline is not met.

1991   **January 9:** James Baker and Tariq Aziz meet in Geneva in final effort for peace.

January 17: Allied planes begin air attack on Baghdad.

February 24: Allied forces begin their ground assault.

February 27: After only 100 hours of ground battle, Kuwait is liberated and temporary cease-fire is declared.

For Further Reading

Ali, Maureen. *The Middle East.* New York: Silver Burdett, 1988.

Chadwick, Frank. *Desert Shield Fact Book.* Berkley: New York, 1991.

Dorr, Robert F. *Desert Shield: The Build-Up: The Complete Story.* Motorbooks: Osceola, WI, 1991.

Gibson, Michael. *Energy Crisis.* New York: Rourke, 1987.

Iraq. New York: Chelsea House, 1988.

Mulloy, Martin. *Kuwait.* New York: Chelsea House, 1988.

Index

Abbasids, 21
Air assaults, 54, 56
Allied forces. *See* Multinational forces
Arab nations
  history of, 23
  Israel and, 7, 10, 14
  military of, 11
  oil and, 14, 17
  poverty in, 17
  United States and, 14
Arab tribes, 16
Arnett, Peter, 56
Assad, Hafez, 38
Assyrians, 21
Aziz, Tariq, 50, 57

Baath party, 24–25, 28
Babylonians, 21
Baghdad, 21, 27, 50
Baker, James, 13, 50
Basra, 29
Blacks, 41
Britain. *See* Great Britain
Bubiyan Island, 19

Bush, George
  hostages and, 39
  Kuwait invasion and, 6
  Kuwait liberation and, 54, 57, 59, 60
  oil and, 13
  Saudi Arabia and, 38
  U.S. military and, 33, 41, 43, 47

Camp David Accords, 10
Carter, Jimmy, 14, 15
Casualties, 56, 58, 60
Chemical weapons, 27
Cheney, Richard, 56
China, 47
Colonialism, 23
Congress, U.S., 13, 43, 47
Constitution, U.S., 43, 47
Cuba, 47

Desert, 46

Economic sanctions, 31–33, 38, 45

Economy, world, 13
Egypt
  history of, 23
  Israel and, 10, 14
  military of, 11, 34, 38
  poverty in, 17
Embargo, oil, 14–15
Emir of Kuwait, 5, 16
Energy, alternative, 15, 17, 19
Environment, 54–55
European nations, 6, 11, 23

Fahd, King, 10, 33–34
Faisal, King, 24
Foreign embassies, 34
France, 11, 23, 34
Friendly fire, 56

Gasoline, 13
Gas crisis (1973), 14
Gas crisis (1979), 14, 15
Gorbachev, Mikhail, 57
Great Britain
  colonialism and, 16, 22, 23, 24

military of, 11, 34
oil and, 16, 17
Soviet plan and, 57
Ground assault, 57–59

Hashemite family, 23
Hope, Bob, 46
Hostages, 34, 36–37, 39,
    49–50
Human rights abuses, 9–10, 57
Human shields, 34, 36–37, 39,
    49–50
Hussein, King, 10
Hussein, Saddam, 28
    Arab world and, 9
    hostages and, 34, 36–37,
        39, 49–50
    Iran-Iraq War and, 27
    Kuwait invasion by, 5, 6, 34
    leadership of, 19, 25, 28, 60
    sanctions against, 33
    war against, 54–60

Iran, 14, 18, 21, 24, 27
Iran-Iraq War, 5, 16, 19,
    27, 29
Iraq
    Arab world and, 7, 9, 10, 38
    assets of, 6
    environment and, 54–55
    history of, 21–29
    human rights in, 9–10
    invasion by, 5–6, 9, 10, 34
    military of, 56, 58–60
    oil and, 13, 18, 19, 32–33
    population of, 27
    religion in, 27
    sanctions against, 31–33,
        38, 45
    size of, 25
    surrender of, 58–60
    war against, 54–60
Islam, 16, 27, 46
Israel, 7, 10, 24, 38, 39, 54

Jefferson, Thomas, 43
Jidda, 29

Jordan, 10, 17, 38, 39

Khafji, 55
Khomeini, Ayatollah Ruholla,
    27
Kurds, 27
Kuwait
    history of, 23
    invasion of, 5-6, 9, 34, 45
    Iran-Iraq War and, 29
Kuwait (continued)
    liberation of, 54–60
    oil and, 13, 16, 17, 18, 19
    religion in, 16
    rulers of, 5, 16
    size of, 6
    wealth of, 17
Kuwait City, 5, 34, 59

League of Nations, 23, 24
Lebanon, 23

Marines, U.S., 41, 42, 56
Mesopotamia, 21
Middle East, 23, 24
Minority groups, 41
Morocco, 34
Multinational forces, 38, 39,
    49, 55, 56
Muslims, 27

National Guard, U.S., 42
Noriega, Manuel, 43
Nuclear weapons, 47

Oil, 11, 13–19, 32–33,
    54–55, 60
Oman, 38
OPEC, 18–19
Operation Desert Shield, 31,
    33, 41, 45, 50
Operation Desert Storm, 41,
    50, 54–59
Organization of Petroleum
    Exporting Countries
    (OPEC), 18–19
Ottoman Empire, 16, 21, 23

Pahlavi, Mohammed Reza, 27
Palestine Liberation
    Organization, 38
Palestinians, 7, 10, 38, 39
Panama, 43
Pan-Arabism, 9
Patriot missiles, 54
Peace efforts, 10, 50, 57
Perez de Cuellar, Javier, 50
Persian Gulf, 17, 54
Poverty, 17
Powell, Colin, 56
Prisoners, 55, 58

Qatar, 55
Quotas, oil production, 19

Refugees, 5, 34, 39
Republican Guard, 58
Reserve combat units, 42
Rumaila oil field, 19

Sabah, Jabir al-Ahmad al-, 5
Sabah family, 16
Saddam. See Hussein, Saddam
Saud family, 10
Saudi Arabia
    Iran-Iraq War and, 29
    Kuwait invasion and, 5, 6,
        38, 45
    oil and, 16, 17, 18, 19
    religion in, 46
    rulers of, 10–11
    wealth of, 17
Schwarzkopf, H. Norman,
    56, 58
Scud missiles, 54, 58
Shatt al-Arab waterway, 27, 29
Shevardnadze, Eduard, 49
Shiite Muslims, 27
Six Day War, 7
Soviet Union. See Union of
    Soviet Socialist Republics
Sumerians, 21
Sunni Muslims, 27
Syria, 11, 14, 23, 34, 38

Television news, 50
Terrorism, 38
Turks, 16, 21, 22, 23

Union of Soviet Socialist
    Republics, 16, 57
United Arab Emirates, 38
United Nations, 35, 57, 60
    military force and, 47, 49
    sanctions by, 6, 31

United States
    Arab nations and, 11, 23, 38
    embassy of, 34
    Kuwait invasion and, 6,
        10, 38
    ·Kuwait liberation and,
        54–60
    military of, 33–34, 41, 46,
        47, 54, 56, 58
    oil and, 13–17
    sanctions by, 32–33

Soviet plan and, 57

Warba Island, 19
War declaration, U.S., 43
Weapons, 27, 47, 51
Women, 41, 46, 55
World economy, 13
World War I, 22
World War, II, 24

Yemen, 17, 38, 47

Photo credits

Cover, p. 4, 37, 40, 51 (Patriot Missile, Stealth Fighter), 52–53, Gamma-Liaison; p. 7, 8, 9, 10, 11, 12, 15, 18, 22, 25, 26, 28, 30, 32, 33, 36, 38, 42, 44, 46, 47, 48, 49, 50, 51 (Apache Helicopter, TOW Anti-tank Missiles, Night-vision Goggles), 59, Wide World Photos, Inc.; p. 20, Art Resource; p. 35, 43, Bruce Glassman.

Maps by Robert Italiano.